Remains Unknown

1 2 3 4 5 6 7 8 9 10 XXX 05 05 04 03 02 01 00 99

Library of Congress Cataloging-in-Publication Data
Caduto, Michael J.
      Remains unknown: the final journey of the human spirit/by
   Michael J. Caduto; illustrated by Adelaide Murphy Tyrol.
                  p. cm.
      ISBN 1-884592-24-4 (cloth).
      1. Funeral rites and ceremonies—Vermont.   2. Burial.   I.
   Tyrol, Adelaide.   II. Title.
GT3210.V5 C33 1999
393'.1'09743—dc21

                                             99-043621

Printed in the United States of America

Text Copyright © 1999 Michael J. Caduto
Illustrations and cover Copyright © 1999 Adelaide Murphy Tyrol
Published by Images from the Past, Inc., Bennington, VT 05201
Tordis Ilg Isselhardt, Publisher

Design and Production: Stillwater Studio
Printer: Thomson-Shore, Inc., Dexter, MI
Text: Utopia with Greymantle MVB drop caps. Display: Pepita.
Paper: 60# Glatfelter Supple Opaque Recycled Natural
Dustjacket: 80# Enamel, printed four process colors plus lamination

Remains Unknown

The Final Journey of a Human Spirit

by Michael J. Caduto

illustrated by
Adelaide Murphy Tyrol

Images from the Past
Bennington, Vermont

for

John & Donna

and

all who dedicate their lives
to healing
and bringing peace
to the spirits
of the forgotten
and the unknown

Remains Unknown

As I drive the shovel down through the thick grass and into the soft, sandy loam, sweat already beading from my brow wrapped in summer's hot, wet afternoon blanket, I pause to look around at the countryside and wonder how I came to be here digging this grave. Just over the stone wall, in the old part of the cemetery, stand hundreds of headstones bearing dates that stretch back beyond the Civil War. Tablets of blue-black slate, white corroded marble, and granites of pink, black, and gray bear the final words by which lives are summed. Beyond, along one of the dirt roads that border two sides of this field of silent gatherings, two young women ride slowly by on chestnut mares. They stare in my direction, but make no effort to rein in their mounts or to cast a query, as if the sight of someone wearing normal street clothes while digging in the local cemetery in the middle of the day is of no consequence.

I work the shovel around the outline of the grave, having estimated the three-foot width and measured the seven-foot height by lying down in the grass and adding a bit more than a foot to my height. Once the boundary is complete, I cut the sod down the middle and section each strip into squares that can be lifted and stacked so they may be replanted in the exact position from which they had been removed. After cutting the last block, I sit back against the wooden rail fence that runs along the north edge of the plot, take a long drink of bottled water, and wait for David to arrive so he can help me dig the hole.

One month ago, while my wife and I were sitting and watching TV, we heard someone knock on the door. We opened it and found our friends, Julia and David, who seemed reluctant to come in. The four of us exchanged greetings, wandered out into the driveway and began to talk.

"We would like your spiritual guidance on something we're working on," said David. "It's perfectly fine if you don't want to get involved with this project, but, because the burial we're working on is for a non-Native person, I immediately thought of you. There's a good chance he may have been Catholic, but we don't know for sure. Do you want to know more, or should we handle it ourselves?"

"Well, sure," I said. "What's going on?"

He pulled out a faded manila envelope, unfolded the metal clasps, and slipped a photograph into my hand. Staring out from that picture was nothing less than an unclothed mummy. His shriveled, leather-like skin hung in sheets draped over bones laced with sinew and dried blood vessels. I was overwhelmed with a deep sadness.

"Who is it?"

"This is the only information we have," said David as he handed me two faded, brittle letters. One, dated September 21, 1896, was addressed to Mr. Frederick L. Wood. It read:

Dear Sir:

Your letter duly received as regards the Skeleton. I came here in March 1873—The skeleton was here then. Handed to Dr. N. D. Peck by Dr. A. N. Mosshell (both are dead). I always understood this was the body of a Mexican Soldier. I cannot tell who the first owner was. I am quite positive Middlebury College never saw it—

Respectfully,
Mrs. Lawrence DeWitt
RD #2
Middlebury, Vt

I looked up from the letter to see David and Julia had lit their pipes and were smoking. For Julia, who is

6

Abenaki, and David, who is an adopt-
ed son, smoking a blend of sage and
tobacco is an act of purification and a
prayer for spiritual clarity. I caught
Julia's eye, which seemed to say, "Go
on, there's more."

So I handed the first letter to Elizabeth and read the second letter,
which was written in Underfield, Vermont on August 24, 1937.

To whom it may concern: —

*On or about June 30, 1936, I
obtained the herein exhibited
skeleton (or mummy) from Mrs.
Lawrence DeWitt of Middlebury,
Vt. Mrs. DeWitt had gathered the
impression that it was the body of
a soldier who was killed in the
Mexican War.*

Estimates by those who have seen this skeleton (or mummy) at my residence place the time of death at from 100 to 150 years ago.

(signed)   Frederick L. Wood

As I handed the second letter to Elizabeth, she looked at me with bewilderment and confusion.

"What else do you know about this person?" I asked.

"I'm afraid that's all the history there is," said David. "We think the body was used for medical research at Middlebury College for a time, then passed on to the old Underfield Medical School, which closed years ago. For the past 25 years or so he has been used for studying anatomy in the Underfield High School biology class."

"What's going on with him now?" I asked.

"The biology teacher's wife came to one of Julia's lectures and, a year later, decided that this guy had to be given a proper burial. You know, one of the talks Julia often gives about the Native belief in the importance of burial and human dignity, and how the body must be at peace before the spirit can make its final journey to the spirit world."

"Wow," I said.

"Whew," agreed Elizabeth.

David continued, "We've been to their house to see him. He's in their garage in a plywood box made especially for him. When we opened the box, Julia knew right away that he was not Native. Then we checked the teeth and confirmed it. He doesn't have the shovel-shaped incisors of a Native person. But he has high cheekbones like yours and we suspect that he may have been Catholic. So I knew you were the person to bring this to."

"Thanks a lot!" I joked.

"Hey, if it's not something you want to…."

"No, no, I'm just kidding. I feel his deep sadness. He wants so much to be at peace. What can I do to help?"

"We thought he should have a Catholic service," Julia added. "Do you know any priests in the area who could be trusted to perform a service quietly, and under these circum-stances?"

"Boy, I can't think of anyone off-hand.... Wait, there is one person who I would trust. He is very connected and has strong roots in the social justice movement of the '60s. He's a great guy with a good sense of humor. I could give him a call."

"These folks are getting antsy with him being in their garage and all," said David. "There's a bit of urgency. Can you call now?"

"Sure, let's get things rolling."

I went into the house and made the call to Father Tomasi. Our cat, Chipmunk, came over and rubbed my leg as I sat down near the phone. She seemed suddenly fragile as I thought that someday she'd look like the photo of the remains I now had etched in my mind. I shook off the image, picked her up, and hugged her to reassure myself, then dialed the number as she purred on my lap.

Reluctantly, I left a message on the answering machine, thinking that it would probably be the strangest message Father Tomasi had received in a long time.

"Hello, Father Tomasi, this is Peter Milano. I hope you are well. There's no crisis, so don't worry, but something important has come up that I could use your help with. It's rather urgent, and I'd appreciate it if you would call me back as soon as possible. Again, it's not life and death or anything, just something I'd like to discuss with you as soon as possible. Please give me a call."

I flipped Chipmunk onto my left shoulder and took her outside with me. "He wasn't in, so I left a message."

"Do you two want to come in and have something to drink?" asked Elizabeth.

"Show-uh," said David.

"Thank you, Elizabeth," Julia replied as the four of us went inside. We sat in the living room chatting for a while when the phone rang.

"Hello."

"Peter, this is Father Tomasi. What's the matter?"

Father Tomasi listened quietly as I told him the story.

"And how do you think I can help?" he asked.

"We think, given the fact that he may be Spanish, and that the dominant religion at the time was Catholicism, perhaps you could perform a simple service at the burial."

"Let's get together and discuss it," he replied. We set up a meeting for the next day, Saturday morning.

After I sit for a time with my back against the rail fence, David and Julia drive up in his Swiss-cheese version of an aging Honda Civic station wagon. Elizabeth had to work that afternoon. "Pietro, you're a good man," says David. "You've already started digging."

"Tabit," I say, using the Abenaki form, "I thought that we could save the sod in squares and replace them in the same order and position that they were in originally. Hi, Julia."

"Let me put the tarp down for the soil," he says. We spread it out on the west side of where we are to dig the grave. Working our shovels together, we lever each square of sod out of the soil and place them sod-side-down on the tarp. Then we start to dig, throwing the dirt up onto the bottom of the sod.

"Crockery shards," says David, who is an ethnohistorian by trade. He hands the piece of white crockery up to Julia.

"I had a feeling this was a dooryard," she says. "The house was probably right over there," she adds, pointing north.

We continue to find bits of crockery as we dig. In time the hole gets too deep for two people to work in, so I continue to dig while David pushes the dirt off to one side and makes room for more soil on the tarp. On the north end of the hole the soil is rocky. One the other end, it is the smoothest, finest sandy loam my shovel has ever bit into.

"This is amazing," I say. "It's like digging in butter."

"Let's leave a bit of a shelf for his head, on the north side," says David.

"Yes, Captain," I reply with a salute.

"You're a good man, Pietro, and you're doing all the work," says David.

"Yeah, right," I protest.

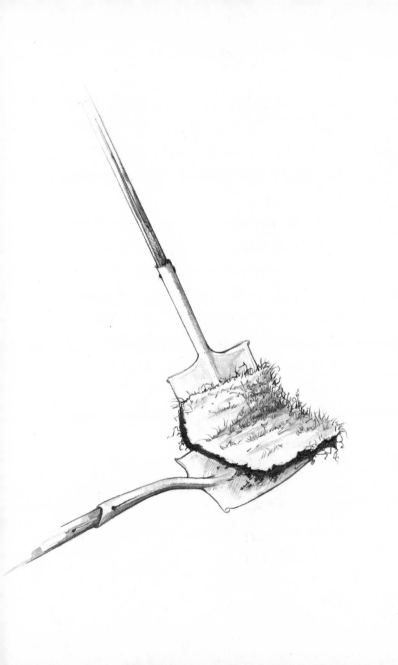

"I don't know why they oriented these new plots to the north-south," says Julia. "We can turn him a bit so his head faces west when we put him in."

The whole time we are digging, cars are driving by, even a policeman. A few people look over, but most do not. We do not look official. We do not look like we belong here, and could be looting a grave in broad daylight. It's as if the passersby look, but cannot see us.

In about an hour, the hole is finished.

"Well, let's see if it's the right size," says David as he starts to climb down inside. "Don't you dare!" screams Julia, as she rises to her feet and grabs the back of his sweat-soaked shirt.

We all light our pipes and smoke silently. Each, in turn, blows smoke down into the hole. Each saying a silent prayer.

Before we parted on Friday night, we agreed to drive to Underfield to look for a suitable burial site the next morning. Then we hugged and said goodnight.

As our friends drove away, I said to Elizabeth, "Well, I'm glad we're going to take care of this person, but, a few hours ago, this is not exactly how I would have said we'd be spending the weekend."

"I know what you mean," she replied.

"I'm kind of excited. It might seem strange, but do you remember when we were driving back from Pennsylvania a few weeks ago, and I was debating whether or not I could keep going on earning a living as a professor of literature?"

"Yeah."

"I had said that, if I could choose to try something totally different I might try being a forensic pathologist—a detective. Well, who would have thought that this experience would present itself a few weeks later?"

The next morning, when David and Julia drove up, we all piled into my Volvo wagon and headed toward

Underfield. On the way, we picked up a fresh-baked loaf of olive bread for Father Tomasi.

"Have either of you had anything come up about this guy since last night?" asked David.

"Just an overwhelming sadness," I said.

"I feel the same," said Elizabeth. "Like he just wants to go home."

"I had a dream of flowers," said Julia. "And of feathers. We're going to find feathers at the burial place."

"When we speak with Father Tomasi," David requested, "let's open slowly to see how much he's willing to take on. I don't want to go too far into things, if he's feeling hesitant."

I parked the car and we walked quietly up the driveway that ran be-

tween the church and the rectory. Father Tomasi greeted us at the door.

"Peter, come in."

"Father, I'd like to you to meet my wife, Elizabeth. This is David and that is Julia."

"Sit down, sit down," he said. "Now, what's going on? I'm afraid I haven't got much time. There's been an unexpected death in the family among some friends of mine and I've got a long ride ahead of me."

David briefed him on all we knew about the history of the remains.

"And what do you envision as being my role in this?" he asked.

"We wanted to ask you if you would perform some kind of service during the burial. We're not sure if he was Catholic."

"No, I don't think he would have been," said Father Tomasi. "We wouldn't have reached them yet at that time and place."

"It doesn't have to be a Catholic service," I explained. "Perhaps a general service to honor his life and send him off on his journey."

"I think I could do something of that nature. But this is highly irregular. If the papers get wind of it they would eat it up. I'm glad to help in a quiet way. But if this thing goes public, I'm out of here."

"Understood," said David.

"We're also looking for an appropriate place to bury him," Julia added. "We pictured someplace where wildflowers grow. A sacred place."

"Well, it's all hallowed ground. Isn't it?" said Father Tomasi.

"Bless you, Father!" said Julia, beaming. "It makes me feel so good to hear you say that."

We drove from the rectory to a cemetery that I thought would be a good possibility. As we got out of the car I said, "This is one of the oldest cemeteries in town. Some of the people buried here go back to the Civil War."

"It has a good feeling," said David. Julia simply got out of the car, lit her pipe, looked around, and wandered over to the gateway. Elizabeth and I walked among the headstones, trying to decide if there was any space left for new burials. After a while, we

walked over to where we saw David and Julia focusing on an unmarked mound just inside the gateway.

"This is it," said Julia as she pointed to the plot. She held up a crow's feather that she'd found on the ground nearby.

"Wow," I said.

As the four of us filed out through the gateway, Elizabeth pointed to a place about six feet up along the bark of a tree. There, stuck in along the edge of a plastic street number nailed to the tree, was a goose feather. "Did you put that there?" Elizabeth asked Julia.

"No, I didn't put that there," Julia replied. "Look at that! Do you believe that?" said Julia as she pointed it out

to David. "I told you there'd be feathers. I know this is the place."

The four of us drove to several
other cemeteries that morning and
early afternoon.

"Too many people," said Julia
about the site in Poundbridge.

"Too noisy!" she exclaimed about
the graveyard in Shelby.

"Do you want to go visit him?"
asked David.

"Yes," I said. "What do you think,
Elizabeth?"

"Sure."

We drove a few miles farther, up a
steep dirt road to a modern, red,
ranch-style house.

David explained, "They told us to
stop by anytime we wanted to see him

as we pieced things together. He's in that box standing in the garage."

We got out of the car and walked in silence to the mouth of the garage.

"Last time we visited he was feeling confined because the lid of the box was latched shut," said David. "So we left the lid leaning open and covered it with a blanket. He also has a sheet over him inside the box." Then, to me and Elizabeth, "Are you ready for this?"

"I think so," I said.

"I guess so," Elizabeth replied.

"Get the other side," said David. Together, we lifted the lid and moved it off to the side. Again the sadness wafted over me.

It was a plunge into a deep pool of grief, dark and foreboding. Then, a call for help to be released. We all looked at his exposed head for a time. During the years when he resided with the medical schools, someone had made a clean horizontal cut and removed his skull cap, which now rested in place. Several three-quarter-inch holes had been drilled in the left side of his skull, probably by a medical student practicing to become a brain surgeon. His cheekbones were indeed high. Light brown eyelashes still fringed the lower edges of his orbits. He was, in fact, a mummy. Yet, despite his age and condition, he stood an impressive six feet tall.

"I want to uncover him to see the rest," I said, "but I feel that would be disrespectful."

Elizabeth and Julia wandered over to the car and sat inside. David and I remained with him for a while.

"I can feel that you are hurting," I said. "We will do everything we can to put you at rest." I held his wrist. "It won't be long now. You will be at peace."

Over the next few weeks, David and I made a number of calls to local officials to check on whether there was space remaining in the cemetery down by the river, how much it would cost, and whether Father Tomasi could meet us on the appointed day. After several false starts and knots in the schedule, we finally got the pieces to fall into place. In recognition of the public nature of the burial, and the service that this man gave to the students of Underfield all those years, the town offered to sell us the cemetery plot for $1.00, instead of the usual $100. David and I were to go the day before and dig the hole. On Wednesday, July 9, David, Julia and I would prepare the body and meet everyone at 3:00 the next day for the burial service.

The day after digging the grave, I drive over to pick up Julia and David. They are preparing for the burial. Julia's car is loaded with satchels of sage, cedar, tobacco, and other gifts. Several boughs of white pine, spruce, and hemlock are tied to the canoe rack.

"How are you doing? Are you ready for this?" asks David.

"I'm doing fine," I reply.

"You can drive over with us if you don't mind sitting in back," says David.

"I can't," I reply. "I get dizzy sitting in the back."

"We're going to need someplace to carry him once we get him ready," Julia observes. "If we take both cars we can put him in the back of Peter's wagon when it's time."

"That would be fine," I say. On the drive over, my thoughts focus on this person, of whom we know so little.

He died more than 135 years ago, and may have been a soldier in the Mexican War. But we don't know that for sure. Perhaps he fought in that war, a war that the Mexicans didn't want, a Federal land grab for the southwestern part of North America that many felt was justified by the country's belief in Manifest Destiny. Mexican families and Native villages were wiped out. People were dispersed. War always breeds refugees. He may have lost his family and found the countryside ravaged.

Where could he go? To the Southeast, and face a life of prejudice, for which that region was well known. Someone told him that, in the Northeast, he might find acceptance, or at least tolerance. People there would allow him to live. So, after a time of wandering and searching, he rode his horse to the north and east, where he

picked up and followed the path of the Underground Railroad. His trail ended, somehow, in Middlebury, Vermont.

He never got used to the cold, bitter winters, and was not fully accepted as one of the locals. With odd jobs as a carpenter, farmhand, pulling down any work he could get, he survived another ten years or so. Near the end, he lived alone in a boardinghouse. One winter, he came down with a cold that wouldn't go away, that turned into a fever and took his life.

Since he was without family, and had been living alone, some researchers at the local medical school gave themselves permission to use him for research. That began the journey of abuse, spiritual pain, and unrest at the end of which he came to be known as "Oscar" by the students of Underfield High School, who, in their fear and anxiety at staring into the face of death, visited all manner of humiliation and derision upon him. It was amazing how students could see the blood vessels preserved; how, in life, the tendons would have pulled each digit like the strings of a puppet; how that same connection looked when they eyed their own living flesh and rolled the fingers up and down. Sinew tying the living to the dead. Dried muscle and bone that could not possibly take this man home. Home to the place from which he had come at birth. Home to be at peace, to meet the family and friends who waited there for him, whom he had not seen for, perhaps, 150 years. Back to where his heart remained, to pick up the beating and rushing of blood that had once been a life among those he knew and loved.

When we arrive at the garage, the biology teacher is there to greet us. We say hello and I notice that he is agitated. He paces and doesn't seem to know what to say. I think it is confusion, the angst that comes when the truth comes up from behind and overtakes you after many years of running. When you realize that everyone else knows your inner secret and you want to crawl into a hole and come out when it is all over and the others have gone home.

"You're welcome to come to the ceremony," says David.

"I'm planning to be there," he says. "I think it's important."

We agree.

After he drives off in his maroon Triumph Spitfire, David, Julia, and I begin to prepare the body. Carefully, we uncover the box and greet him. He stands as he always has, with arms in an awkward, reaching pose, as if gesturing, "Help me."

"It's going to be all right. It's time to go home. We apologize for the pain this may cause, but this is the last part of your journey."

We lift the box, with him inside, and lay it on its back. Then we spread the burial cloth next to the box. Carefully, we remove the screws and wires

45

that have imprisoned him for a century. When he is free, we gently lift him out of the box and onto the burial cloth. Julia waits silently by—smoking, praying, sussing the next steps and guiding us. We talk to him, calm him, console him as we work. At last, snipping here, twisting there, we remove every screw, each bit of wire, and lay his limbs, as best we can, comfortably by his side. Every morsel of waste is saved for burial.

Now we need to cover him with sage, cedar, and tobacco to send him on the blessing way. David shows how. I follow. Our friend's sense of fear seems to ease, he seems to relax now, as if, for the first time, he realizes that this is the final indignity that he will have to suffer, that it is near time to

go home. We tie his skull cap securely in place and wrap him. Darkness, rest.

"Let's put him in head first," says David. I go over to the back seat and help lift him in place. "Don't close the trunk just yet; leave it open a bit so he can breathe. We have to go bury the remains of the remains."

"What about the box?" I ask.

"The teacher told us to put it on top of the brush pile so he could burn it later on," says David. Then, carefully, as if carrying a piece of old furniture, we ease the box up over some stone steps, across a brief patch of lawn, and over to the brush pile at the edge of the field. Unceremoniously, we heave the box atop the tangle of tree branches and lawn clippings.

"He's not going to miss that thing," I say. "It's been his prison for far too long." On the way back across the lawn I point out the thick patches of sulfur-colored cinquefoil growing amid the sparse clumps of grass.

In a gentle rain, David and I walk around the side of the garage. A swallow flies over. "I have been seeing lots of swallows and finches the past few weeks, whenever I've been thinking about this burial," I say.

We walk down the steep slope to the broad stream below. David buries the wires, my gloves, and the tidbits that we found in the bottom of his box. We wash and pray. I ask for the right words, for the respect and clarity to make his journey to the cemetery a

good one. We each wash our face with the cleansing waters.

"You're a good man to help us," says David.

Always a bit embarrassed when he says this, I reply, "And you, my friend. It's good work that we're doing."

On the way up, we remark on the wild ginger growing along the stream-bank.

David and Julia pull out of the driveway ahead of me, leading the way and clearing a path. David stops suddenly, gets out, and comes back to my car.

"Don't forget to talk to him on the way over," he says.

"I won't," I assure him.

So I comfort this stranger who makes his final journey in my car. "You're going home now. You are finally going to be at peace. It's a beautiful day for traveling. We're going to go over the ridge. Your resting place is magnificent; the river flows just below. It's quiet and green there."

David stops their car and Julia gets out to pick some daisies and other flowers for a bouquet.

I get out and walk over to his window. "Hey, David, is this the traditional way? The man sits behind the wheel while the woman gets out and does all the work?"

"Absolutely, Peter!" calls Julia, who overhears from in the field. "What do you think?"

We continue driving. I flash my lights and pull ahead of their car so they will follow me down a shortcut. I stop along Oxbow Road to pick some Queen Anne's lace. "This would have been growing in his ancestors' native land," I say.

On the last leg of the drive, I continue to talk to him, then I play him a song, "So Strong Your Love," from the Song in Our Silence album recorded by the Brothers of the Weston Priory. As the ending notes ring out, we make the turn toward the cemetery. I can feel his excitement growing as we near. "This is it," I say. "You're almost home."

I back the car in and wait, with David and Julia, for the others to arrive. David and I lay the spruce, pine,

and hemlock boughs down in the bottom of the grave. Julia smokes.

They ride into town to get a balsam pillow for his head. I smoke quietly, alone. I lean over the edge of the grave and blow thick puffs in the still, thick afternoon air. They waft down and mingle with the pungent needles. The smoke seems to catch there, trapped for some time among the boughs, slowly breathing with the needles themselves. I'm glad for this time alone.

David and Julia return. Elizabeth arrives from work. People come quickly: the manager of town cemeteries, the biology teacher, and, finally, Father Tomasi. We greet everyone and thank them for coming. The biology teacher has a small bouquet of field wildflowers that he picked along the way. Clutching the stems in his thick fist he walks self-consciously to where the soldier lies beside the grave, leans over, and gently places the flowers upon the soldier's shrouded chest. He stands up and stares, mesmerized. Silently, we all gather around the edge of the grave.

The service begins as Father Tomasi sprinkles the soldier with holy water. Beautiful words ensue which embrace the hands of faith that have brought this man to the last portal.

"Let us pray. We face death again, Father, and, as always, it is new and fresh and painful. Always it means mystery and fear for us, as well as separation. Yet in your Son, our Lord and

brother, you have made us one, and his promise of a risen life where we will be free at last rings in our hearts and gives us a strong taste for hope. We pray then for our brother, and for ourselves and all the dying that the life we know so well may be pale beside the life that we shall see.

"Lord Jesus Christ, by your own three days in the tomb, you hallowed the graves of all who believe in you and so made the grave a sign of hope that promises resurrection even as it claims our mortal bodies. Grant that our brother may sleep here in peace until you awaken him to glory. Then he will see you face to face and in your light will see light and know the splendor of God, for you live and reign for ever and ever.

"Into your hands, Father of mercies, we commend our brother in the sure and certain hope that, together with all who have died in Christ, he will rise with him on the last day. May you grant him mercy and pardon his sins. Merciful Lord, turn toward us and listen to our prayers. Open the gates of Paradise to your servant and help us who remain to comfort one another with assurances of faith, until we all meet in Christ and are with you, with all the saints and with our brother forever. Amen."

Unexpectedly, the teacher begins to sob. I now see that this healing touches more lives than I realized. I feel small in my ignorance, and blessed to be here to see this honest

release. The catharsis rolls over us and we move closer to the teacher to console him. Now the circle is complete. The rest will come to all, in this world, and the next.

"It is good that you came today," David says to the teacher.

"I knew I had to be here," he says between tears.

Father Tomasi looks at David and me and we pick up our cue. Slowly, we lift the body into the grave. As we lower him, the feet and head touch the ends of the grave. He bends a little. I look at David. "The hole is short by about six inches. Let's lift him out and I'll get the shovel."

A little discomfort, some dark humor rises up among us. I think to myself, "I'll bet Father Tomasi has never had this happen at one of his funerals before!" In a few, short minutes, my shovel carves the hole about eight inches longer. We lower him down at a slight angle and he fits easily.

"Would you like to be the first?" David says to the teacher. He walks over and begins to shovel soil onto the body. He does this with unexpected, unabashed enthusiasm.

"I don't blame him," I think to myself. "He's probably relieved to arrive at this point in his own journey."

Taking turns, we fill the hole. The biology teacher's wife arrives from work, just in time to see the process she started in motion many weeks ago come to fruition.

"Mound the soil up a few inches," says David. "Believe me, it's going to settle a lot."

David and I replace the sod, putting each piece back exactly where we found it. With care, I use handfuls of soil to fill the cracks between pieces of sod, raking the excess with my fingers. After we finish, there is a good pile of soil left on the tarp. All pulling together, we are just able to drag it over the grass and down to the roadside, where we spread it out. There, for the first time, we loosen up a bit and begin to joke around. A little banter, some history and stories from the teacher.

"When I first arrived at the school, the biology teacher whom I was replacing had put this man's box in the hallway with a sign on it that said 'Please take to the dump.' I could see that was wrong, that this was something important. At the very least, we could use it to study anatomy in our classes." He continues with other stories, relieving his burden. We suddenly realize that he was the one who first began the acts of value that led us to be here helping to complete the circle of this man's life on this hot July afternoon. After saying our good-byes and thank-you's, the four of us remain: David, Julia, Elizabeth, and me.

Julia goes over to the grave and smokes again. She builds a small stone circle over his heart. It is the symbol of completion that we are all gently glad to see. Silently, and aloud,

we all say our last words, then we go off to have something to eat.

Some weeks later, Elizabeth and I return to the cemetery to visit our friend. We notice that the grass on the north half of the grave has grown in lush and green, while much of the grass covering the south end, although sprouting back, has died.

"I was hoping it would be nice and thick, so that you couldn't even tell we'd been here," I say.

"But it's growing back in," says Elizabeth. "It will be fine."

We each say a silent hello and pray our silent prayers.

It is quiet now. I sense that he has gone, that he left soon after we departed on the day we buried him. He was anxious to be on his way; happy to go home. He had been gone for many long lonely years and was sorely missed.

Here lies
a giving spirit
who remains unknown
ca. 1860

IMAGES FROM THE PAST

Publishing history in ways that
help people see it for themselves

ALLIGATORS ALWAYS DRESS FOR DINNER:
An Alphabet Book of Vintage Photographs

By Linda Donigan and Michael Horwitz

A collection of late 19th- and early 20th-century images from around the world reproduced in rich duotone for children and all who love historical pictures. Each two-page spread offers a surprising visual treat: Beholding Beauty—a beautifully dressed and adorned Kikuyu couple; Fluted Fingers—a wandering Japanese Zen monk playing a bamboo recorder; and Working the Bandwagon—the Cole Brothers Band on an elaborate 1879 circus wagon. A-Z information pages with image details.

9 1/4" x 9 3/4", 64 pages   ISBN 1-884592-08-2   Cloth $25.00

LETTERS TO VERMONT Volumes I and II:

From Her Civil War Soldier Correspondents to the Home Press

Donald Wickman, Editor/Compiler

In their letters "To the Editor" of the *Rutland Herald,* young Vermont soldiers tell of fighting for the Union, galloping around Lee's army in Virginia, garrisoning the beleaguered defenses of Washington, D.C., and blunting Pickett's desperate charge at Gettysburg. One writer is captured, another serves as a prison camp guard, others are wounded—and one dies fighting in the horrific conflict in the Wilderness of Virginia. Biographical information for each writer (except one who remains an enigma) and supporting commentary on military affairs. 54 engravings and prints, 32 contemporary maps, 45 historical photographs. Extensive index.

Vol. 1, 6" x 9", 251 pages ISBN 1-884592-10-4 Cloth $30.00
ISBN 1-884592-11-2 Paper $19.95

Vol. 2, 6" x 9", 265 pages ISBN 1-884592-16-3 Cloth $30.00
ISBN 1-884592-17-1 Paper $19.95

REMEMBERING GRANDMA MOSES

By Beth Moses Hickok

Grandma Moses, a crusty, feisty, upstate New York farm wife and grand-mother, as remembered in affectionate detail by Beth Moses Hickok, who married into the family at 22, and raised two of Grandma's granddaughters. Set in 1934, before the artist was "discovered," the book includes family snapshots, and photographs that evoke the landscape of Eagle Bridge, home for most of her century-plus life. Two portraits of Grandma Moses—a 1947 painting and a 1949 photograph, and nine historical photographs. On the cover is a rare colorful yarn painting given to the author as a wedding present.

6" x 9", 64 pages ISBN 1-884592-01-5 Paperback $12.95

AMERICA'S SONG: The Story of Yankee Doodle

By Stuart Murray

During the first uncertain hours of the Revolution, British redcoats sang "Yankee Doodle" as an insult to Americans—but when the rebels won astounding victories this song of insult was transformed to a song of triumph, eventually becoming "America's Song."

This is the first complete chronicle of the story of "Yankee Doodle," perhaps the best-known tune in all the world. From its early days an ancient air for dancing, through the era of Dutch and Puritan colonial settlement, "Yankee Doodle" evolved during the French and Indian Wars and the American Revolution to become our most stirring anthem of liberty. Index. Bibliography. Illustrated with 37 prints and maps.

5" x 7", 248 pages ISBN 1-884592-18-X Cloth $21.00

WASHINGTON'S FAREWELL TO HIS OFFICERS:
After Victory in the Revolution

By Stuart Murray

In the sunlit Long Room of Fraunces Tavern, on a winter's day in New York City, 1783, George Washington's few remaining officers anxiously await his arrival. He has called them here to say goodbye—likely never to see them again. The British redcoats have sailed away, defeated in the Revolution. This moving incident, one almost forgotten in American history, was among the most telling and symbolic events of the War for Independence.

As they anticipate their beloved general's arrival, the officers recall how their struggle for the sacred cause flickered, almost went out, then flared into final victory. In the story of Washington's Farewell are the memories of long-struggling patriots—the famous and the little-known—men committed heart and soul to the cause of American liberty: Knox, McDougall, Lamb, Hamilton, Steuben, Shaw, Humphreys, Varick, Burnett, Hull, Fish, Tallmadge, the Clintons, Van Cortlandt, Fraunces. . . . Heroes all. Index. Bibliography. 42 prints and maps.

5" x 7", 240 pages ISBN 10884592-20-1 Cloth $21.00

RUDYARD KIPLING IN VERMONT:
Birthplace of The Jungle Books

By Stuart Murray

This book fills a gap in the biographical coverage of the important British author who is generally described as having lived only in India and England. It provides the missing links in the bittersweet story that haunts the portals of Naulakha, the distinctive shingle-style home built by Kipling and his American wife near Brattleboro, Vermont. Here the Kiplings lived for four years and the first two of their three children were born.

All but one of Kipling's major works stem from these years of rising success, happiness, and productivity; but because of a feud with his American brother-in-law, Beatty, which was seized on by newspaper reporters eager to put a British celebrity in his place, the author and his family left their home in America forever in 1896.

6" x 9", 208 pages, extensive index. Excerpts from Kipling poems, 21 historical photos, 6 book illustrations, and 7 sketches convey the mood of the times, character of the people, and style of Kipling's work.

ISBN 1-884592-04-X Cloth $29.00
ISBN 1-884592-05-8 Paperback $18.95

THE HONOR OF COMMAND:
Gen. Burgoyne's Saratoga Campaign

By Stuart Murray

Leaving Quebec in June, Burgoyne was confident in his ability to strike a decisive blow against the rebellion in the colonies. Instead, the stubborn rebels fought back, slowed his advance, and inflicted irreplaceable losses, leading to his defeat and surrender at Saratoga on October 17, 1777—an important turning point in the American Revolution. Burgoyne's point of view as the campaign progresses is expressed from his dispatches, addresses to his army, and exchanges with friends and fellow officers. 33 prints and engravings, 8 maps, 10 sketches. Index.

7"x10", 128 pages ISBN 1-884-592-03-1 Paperback $14.95

NORMAN ROCKWELL AT HOME IN VERMONT:
The Arlington Years, 1939-1953

By Stuart Murray

Norman Rockwell painted some of his greatest works, including "The Four Freedoms," during the 15 years he and his family lived in Arlington, Vermont. Compared to his former home in the suburbs of New York City, it was "like living in another world," and completely transformed his already successful career as America's leading illustrator. For the first time he began to paint pictures that "grew out of the every day life of my neighbors."

32 historical photographs, 13 Rockwell paintings and sketches, and personal recollections. Index. Regional map, selected bibliography, and listing of area museums and exhibitions.

7" x 10", 96 pages ISBN 1-884592-02-3 Paperback $14.95

THE ESSENTIAL GEORGE WASHINGTON:
Two Hundred Years of Observations
on the Man, Myth and Patriot

By Peter Hannaford

Why did Thomas Paine turn against him? Why did Elizabeth Powel call him "impudent"? What is the truth about the cherry tree story? What was his single most important quality? These and many more questions about the man called "the father of his country" are answered in this collection. The reader meets Washington's contemporaries, followed by famous Americans from the many decades between then and now and, finally, well-known modern-day Americans. Included are Benjamin Franklin, Thomas Jefferson, Abigail Adams, Parson Weems, Abraham Lincoln, Walt Whitman, Woodrow Wilson, Bob Dole, George McGovern, Eugene McCarthy, Letitia Baldrige, Newt Gingrich, Ronald Reagan—and many more. Read in small doses or straight through...either way, the book gives a full portrait of the man who—more than any other—made the United States of America possible. Over 60 prints and photographs.

5" x 7", 200 pages ISBN 1-884592-23-6 Cloth $19.50

Available at your local bookstore or from Images from the Past, Inc.,

888-442-3204 for credit card orders;

P.O. Box 137, Bennington, Vermont 05201 with check or money order.

When ordering, please add $4.00 shipping and handling
for the first book and $1 for each additional.

(Add 5% sales tax for shipments to Vermont.)

www.ImagesfromthePast.com